Certified Authorization Professional (CAP) Last Minute Review

David Boone

ISBN: 1500884618
ISBN-13: 978-1500884611

DEDICATION

To all the Brave Souls attempting IT security Exams of any flavor.

CONTENTS

ACKNOWLEDGMENTS

To the NIST family of publications for providing superlative process for IT security, many thanks.

1 INTRODUCTION

The ISC2 Certified Authorization Professional (CAP) exam is a 3 hour long multiple choice exam that tests for the ability to pick <u>the best answer</u>, may not necessarily be the only correct answer.   This last minute cram is suitable for quick review of crucial facts and figures. The absolutely essential facts that "must know backwards and forwards" are all in here.   There is no point in attempting the exam without these but <u>by itself is not sufficient to pass.</u>

The contents are organized into different sections, no particular order or logic of materials is presupposed, each factoid is as important as any other in here.   <u>Much of the content are directly taken from the NIST/OMB/Congressional Law publications in the public domain as of 2014 – the value of this work is in zeroing in on some of those vital parts needed to pass the CAP in the thousands of pages of Government-speak to drill down to the essential parts</u>

2 CRUCIAL PUBLICATIONS LIST AND LAWS

CNSS Instruction 1253a	Instruction No. 1253, *Security Categorization and Control Selection for National Security Systems*, provides all Federal Government departments, agencies, bureaus, and offices with guidance on the first two steps of the Risk Management Framework (RMF), Categorize and Select, for national security systems (NSS).
FIPS 199	FIPS Publication 199—to develop standards for categorizing information and information systems. Security categorization standards for information and information systems provide a common framework and understanding for expressing security (High, Medium, Low)
FIPS 200	This standard addresses the specification of minimum security requirements for federal information and information systems The minimum security requirements cover seventeen security-related areas with regard to protecting the confidentiality, integrity, and availability of federal information systems and the information processed, stored, and transmitted by those systems. The security-related areas include: (i) access control; (ii) awareness and training; (iii) audit and accountability; (iv) certification, accreditation, and security assessments; (v) configuration management; (vi) contingency planning; (vii) identification and authentication; (viii) incident response; (ix) maintenance; (x) media protection; (xi) physical and environmental protection; (xii) planning; (xiii) personnel security; (xiv) risk assessment; (xv) systems and services acquisition; (xvi) system and communications protection; and (xvii) system and information integrity.
SP 800-30	The purpose of Special Publication 800-30 is to provide guidance for conducting risk assessments of federal information systems and organizations, amplifying the guidance in Special Publication 800-39. Risk assessments, carried out at all three tiers in the risk management hierarchy, are part of an overall risk management process
SP 800-37	The core, important publication describing the Risk Management Framework in detail
SP 800-39	The purpose of Special Publication 800-39 is to provide guidance for an integrated, organization-wide program for managing information security risk to organizational operations (i.e., mission, functions, image, and reputation), organizational assets, individuals, other organizations, and the Nation resulting from the operation and use of federal information systems.
SP 800-53	The purpose of this publication is to provide guidelines for selecting and specifying security controls for organizations and information systems supporting the executive agencies of the federal government to meet the requirements of FIPS Publication 200, *Minimum Security Requirements for Federal Information and Information Systems*
SP 800-60	Federal Information Processing Standard 199 (FIPS 199), *Standards for Security Categorization of Federal Information and Information Systems*, defines the security categories, security

	objectives, and impact levels to which SP 800-60 maps information types
SP 800-64	The National Institute of Standards and Technology (NIST) Special Publication (SP) 800-64, *Security Considerations in the System Development Life Cycle*, has been developed to assist federal government agencies in integrating essential information technology (IT) security steps into their established IT system development life cycle (SDLC).
SP 800-137	Information security continuous monitoring (ISCM) is defined as maintaining ongoing awareness of information security, vulnerabilities, and threats to support organizational risk management decisions.
Section 3541 Title 44 USC	Federal Information Security Management Act 2002 - Compels the Government to secure its IT resources
OMB Circular A-130	This Appendix establishes a minimum set of controls to be included in Federal automated information security programs; assigns Federal agency responsibilities for the security of automated information; and links agency automated information security programs and agency management control systems established in accordance with OMB Circular No. A-123
OMB Circular A-123	This Circular provides guidance to Federal managers on improving the accountability and effectiveness of Federal programs and operations by establishing, assessing, correcting, and reporting on internal control. The attachment to this Circular defines management's responsibilities related to internal control and the process for assessing internal control effectiveness along with a summary of the significant changes
5 USC 552a	Privacy Act 1974- The Privacy Act of 1974, 5 U.S.C. § 552a, establishes a code of fair information practices that governs the collection, maintenance, use, and dissemination of information about individuals that is maintained in systems of records by federal agencies. A system of records is a group of records under the control of an agency from which information is retrieved by the name of the individual or by some identifier assigned to the individual

FISMA

-Agencies must maintain and information systems inventory

-Agencies must categorize all their information systems per FIPS 199 and SP 800-60

-Agencies must meet minimum security requirements by implementing and assessing security controls per FIPS 200 and SP 800-53 – since SP 800-53 references SP 800-37, it renders it compulsory as well along with a range of other NIST Special Publications, however Agencies have latitude with respect to how they will comply

-Agencies must engage in information system authorization per OMB Circular A-130

Adequate Security [OMB Circular A-130,	Security commensurate with the risk and the magnitude of harm resulting from the loss, misuse, or unauthorized access to or modification of information. This

Appendix III] includes assuring that systems and applications used by the agency operate effectively and provide appropriate confidentiality, integrity, and availability, through the use of cost-effective management, personnel, operational, and technical controls.

3 RISK TIERS

Risk Management Tiers

SP 800-37 Rev 1 emphasizes 3 tiers of risk management including Tier 1 - organizational risk. This tier is where the global institutional risk policies are articulated by the risk executive – framing the risk – establishing the larger conceptual process – the fundamental contexts such a governance structures, larger views of risk tolerance and so on. Tier 1 is about defining a risk strategy for the whole organization –

(i) the techniques and methodologies the organization plans to employ to assess information system related security risks and other types of risk of concern to the organization; (ii) the methods and procedures the organization plans to use to evaluate the significance of the risks identified during the risk assessment; (iii) the types and extent of risk mitigation measures the organization plans to employ to address identified risks; (iv) the level of risk the organization plans to accept (i.e., risk tolerance); (v) how the organization plans to monitor risk on an ongoing basis given the inevitable changes to organizational information systems and their environments of operation; and (vi) the degree and type of oversight the organization plans to use to ensure that the risk management strategy is being effectively carried out.

At Tier 2 the mission and business process layer the enterprise architecture is crucial – the idea is to begin to translate the risk strategy defined in Tier 1 into the sinews of the organization but not at the lowest system level unit but at a higher level of abstraction. For example defining security requirements broadly for an entire organization and at department levels, say sales, happens here. Or, deciding to treat the R&D as its own separate autonomous division with its own unique information inflow and outflow.

Tier 3 is the familiar system unit level where various controls are implemented with Tier 2 security requirements and categorizations in mind.

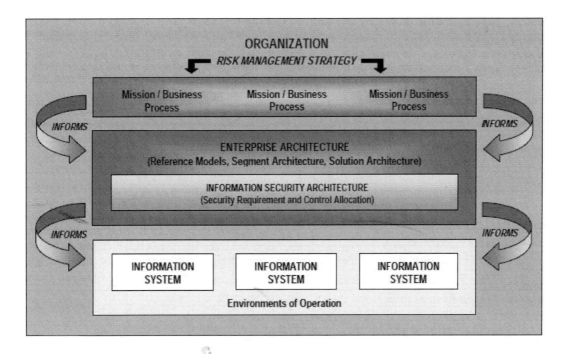

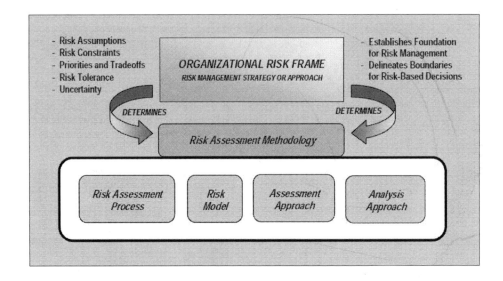

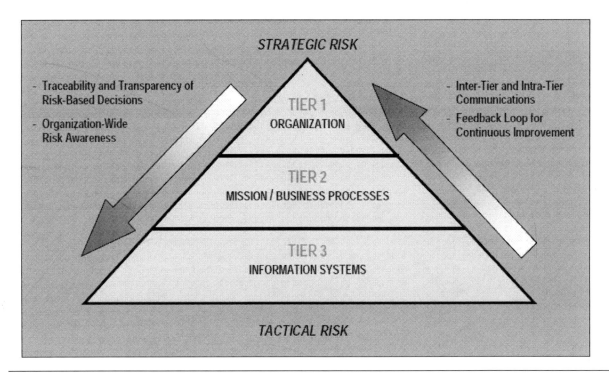

System Inventory and Boundaries

The goal is to identify systems requiring protection, planning, and management.   It is a precursor to authorization but aspects of it can be used in RMF Step 1 categorization.   Circular A-130 describes **general support system** as set of technology resources sharing the same management and common functionality.   **Major application** is a set of IT resources that require special security attention due to the harm that would ensue if their confidentiality, integrity or availability were compromised.   One can create authorization boundaries out of general support and major systems by considering commonality of business purpose, security perimeter and finally ownership

Information system boundaries are established in coordination with the security categorization process and before the development of security plans. Information system boundaries that are too expansive (i.e., too many system components and/or unnecessary architectural complexity) make the risk management process extremely unwieldy and complex. Boundaries that are too limited increase the number of information systems that must be separately managed and as a consequence, unnecessarily inflate the total information security costs for the organization.

The set of information resources[29] allocated to an information system defines the boundary for that system. Organizations have significant flexibility in determining what constitutes an information system and its associated boundary. If a set of information resources is identified as an information system, the resources are generally under the same direct management control.

Complex Systems and Boundaries

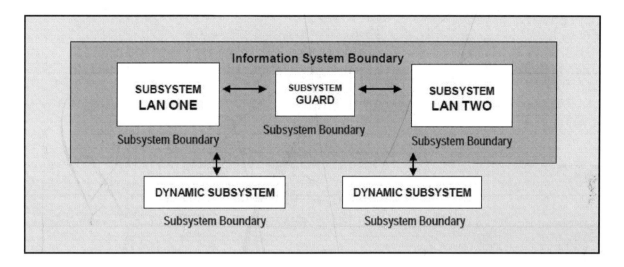

Changes to current information technologies and computing paradigms add complications to the traditional tasks of establishing information system boundaries and protecting the missions and business processes supported by organizational information systems. In particular, net-centric architectures[39] (e.g., service-oriented architectures [SOAs], cloud computing) introduce two important concepts: (i) *dynamic subsystems*; and (ii) *external subsystems*.

Types of Authorization

Organizations can choose from three different approaches when planning for and conducting security authorizations to include: (i) an authorization with a *single* authorizing official; (ii) an authorization with *multiple* authorizing officials; or (iii) *leveraging* an existing authorization

The first approach is the traditional authorization process defined in this appendix where a single organizational official in a senior leadership position is both responsible and accountable for an information system
The second approach, or *joint authorization*, is employed when multiple organizational officials either from the same organization or different organizations, have a shared interest in authorizing an information system. The organizational officials collectively are responsible and accountable for the information system and jointly accept the information system-related security risks

The final approach, *leveraged authorization*, is employed when a federal agency[79] chooses to accept some or all of the information in an existing authorization package generated by another federal agency (hereafter referred to as the *owning* organization[80]) based on a need to use the same information resources (e.g., information system and/or services provided by the system). The leveraging organization reviews the owning organization's authorization package as the basis for determining risk to the leveraging organization

4 RISK MANAGEMENT FRAMEWORK (RMF)

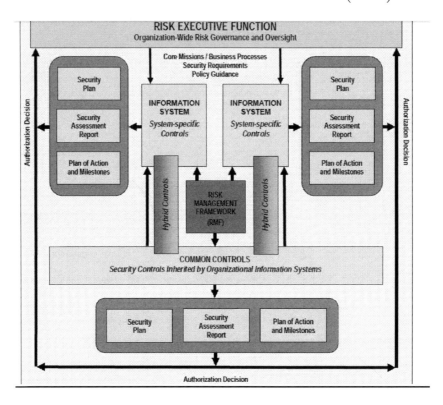

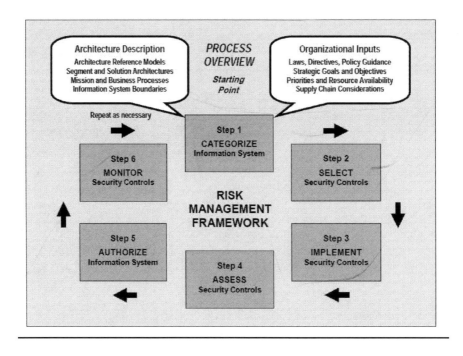

RMF Steps

RMF primarily operates in Tier 3 but disseminates information <u>up the chain</u> to Tier 2 and 3.

RMF STEP 1 – CATEGORIZE INFORMATION SYSTEM

TASK 1-1: Categorize the information system and document the results of the security categorization in the security plan

Primary Responsibility: Information System Owner; Information Owner/Steward.

System Development Life Cycle Phase: Initiation (concept/requirements definition).

References: FIPS Publication 199; NIST Special Publications 800-30, 800-39, 800-59, 800-60; CNSS Instruction 1253.

The security categorization process is conducted as an organization-wide activity taking into consideration the enterprise architecture and the information security architecture. This helps to ensure that individual information systems are categorized based on the mission and business objectives of the organization. The results of the security categorization process influence the selection of appropriate security controls for the information system and also, where applicable, the minimum assurance requirements for that system.

TASK 1-2: Describe the information system (including system boundary) and document the description in the security plan.

Primary Responsibility: Information System Owner.

System Development Life Cycle Phase: Initiation (concept/requirements definition).

Descriptive information about the information system is documented in the *system identification* section of the security plan, included in attachments to the plan, or referenced in other standard sources for information generated as part of the system development life cycle. Many diverse things can be included here such as-

-Full descriptive name of the information system including associated acronym;
- Unique information system identifier (typically a number or code);
- Information system owner and authorizing official including contact information;
-Status of the information system with respect to acquisition and/or system development life cycle;
- Results of the security categorization process for the information and information system;
- Types of information processed, stored, and transmitted by the information system;
- Boundary of the information system for risk management and security authorization purposes;
- Applicable laws, directives, policies, regulations, or standards affecting the security of the information system;
- Architectural description of the information system including network topology;
- Hardware and firmware devices included within the information system;
- System and applications software resident on the information system;
- Hardware, software, and system interfaces (internal and external);
- Subsystems (static and dynamic) associated with the information system;
- Information flows and paths (including inputs and outputs) within the information system;

TASK 1-3: Register the information system with appropriate organizational program/management offices.

Primary Responsibility: Information System Owner.

System Development Life Cycle Phase: Initiation (concept/requirements definition)

Information system registration, in accordance with organizational policy, uses information in the system identification section of the security plan to inform the parent or governing organization of: (i) the existence of the information system; (ii) the key characteristics of the system; and (iii) any security implications for the organization due to the ongoing operation of the system. Information system registration provides organizations with an effective management/tracking tool that is necessary for security

status reporting in accordance with applicable laws, Executive Orders, directives, policies, standards, guidance, or regulations.

RMF STEP 2 – SELECT SECURITY CONTROLS

TASK 2-1: Identify the security controls that are provided by the organization as common controls for organizational information systems and document the controls in a security plan (or equivalent document).

Primary Responsibility: Chief Information Officer or Senior Information Security Officer; Information Security Architect; Common Control Provider.

System Development Life Cycle Phase: Initiation (concept/requirements definition).

References: FIPS Publications 199, 200; NIST Special Publications 800-30, 800-53; CNSS Instruction 1253.

Common controls are security controls that are inherited by one or more organizational information systems. Common controls are identified by the chief information officer and/or senior information security officer in collaboration with the information security architect and assigned to specific organizational entities (designated as common control providers) for development, implementation, assessment, and monitoring. Common control providers may also be *information system owners* when the common controls are resident within an information system. The organization consults information system owners when identifying common controls to ensure that the security capability provided by the inherited controls is sufficient to deliver adequate protection. When the common controls provided by the organization are not sufficient for information systems inheriting the controls, the system owners supplement the common controls with system-specific or hybrid controls to achieve the required protection for the system and/or accept greater risk.

TASK 2-2: Select the security controls for the information system and document the controls in the security plan.

Primary Responsibility: Information Security Architect; Information System Owner.

System Development Life Cycle Phase: Initiation (concept/requirements definition).

References: FIPS Publications 199, 200; NIST Special Publications 800-30, 800-53; CNSS Instruction 1253.

The security controls are selected based on the security categorization of the information system. The security control selection process includes, as appropriate: (i) choosing a set of baseline security controls; (ii) tailoring the baseline security controls by applying scoping, parameterization, and compensating control guidance; (iii) supplementing the tailored baseline security controls, if necessary, with additional controls and/or control enhancements to address unique organizational needs based on a risk assessment (either formal or informal) and local conditions including environment of operation, organization-specific security requirements, specific threat information, cost-benefit analyses, or special circumstances; and (iv) specifying minimum assurance requirements, as appropriate.

TASK 2-3: Develop a strategy for the continuous monitoring of security control effectiveness and any proposed or actual changes to the information system and its environment of operation.

Primary Responsibility: Information System Owner or Common Control Provider.

System Development Life Cycle Phase: Initiation (concept/requirements definition).

References: NIST Special Publications 800-30, 800-39, 800-53; 800-53A; CNSS Instruction 1253

A critical aspect of risk management is the ongoing monitoring of security controls employed within or inherited by the information system. An effective monitoring strategy is developed early in the system development life cycle (i.e., during system design or COTS procurement decision) and can be included in the security plan. The implementation of a robust continuous monitoring program allows an organization to understand the security state of the information system over time and maintain the initial security authorization in a highly dynamic environment of operation with changing threats, vulnerabilities, technologies, and missions/business functions

TASK 2-4: Review and approve the security plan.

Primary Responsibility: Authorizing Official or Designated Representative

System Development Life Cycle Phase: Development/Acquisition.

References: NIST Special Publications 800-30, 800-53; CNSS Instruction 1253.

The independent review of the security plan by the authorizing official or designated representative with support from the senior information security officer, chief information officer, and risk executive (function), helps determine if the plan is complete, consistent, and satisfies the stated security requirements for the information system. The security plan review also helps to determine, to the greatest extent possible with available planning or operational documents, if the security plan correctly and effectively identifies the potential risk to organizational operations and assets, individuals, other organizations, and the Nation, that would be incurred if the controls identified in the plan were implemented as intended.

RMF STEP 3 – IMPLEMENT SECURITY CONTROLS

TASK 3-1: Implement the security controls specified in the security plan.

Primary Responsibility: Information System Owner or Common Control Provider.

System Development Life Cycle Phase: Development/Acquisition; Implementation.

References: FIPS Publication 200; NIST Special Publications 800-30, 800-53, 800-53A; CNSS Instruction 1253; Web: SCAP.NIST.GOV.

Security control implementation is consistent with the organization's enterprise architecture and information security architecture. The information security architecture serves as a resource to allocate security controls (including, for example, security mechanisms and services) to an information system and any organization defined subsystems. Security controls targeted for deployment within the information system (including subsystems) are allocated to specific system components responsible for providing a particular security capability. Not all security controls need to be allocated to every subsystem.

TASK 3-2: Document the security control implementation, as appropriate, in the security plan, providing a functional description of the control implementation (including planned inputs, expected behavior, and expected outputs).

Primary Responsibility: Information System Owner or Common Control Provider.

System Development Life Cycle Phase: Development/Acquisition; Implementation.

References: NIST Special Publication 800-53; CNSS Instruction 1253.

Security control documentation describes how system-specific, hybrid, and common controls are implemented. The documentation formalizes plans and expectations regarding the overall functionality of the information system. The functional description of the security control implementation includes planned inputs, expected behavior, and expected outputs where appropriate, typically for those technical controls that are employed in the hardware, software, or firmware components of the information system.

RMF STEP 4 – ASSESS SECURITY CONTROLS

TASK 4-1: Develop, review, and approve a plan to assess the security controls.

Primary Responsibility: Security Control Assessor.

System Development Life Cycle Phase: Development/Acquisition; Implementation.

References: NIST Special Publication 800-53A.

The *security assessment plan* provides the objectives for the security control assessment, a detailed roadmap of how to conduct such an assessment, and assessment procedures. The assessment plan reflects the type of assessment the organization is conducting (e.g., developmental testing and evaluation, independent verification and validation, assessments supporting security authorizations or reauthorizations, audits, continuous monitoring, assessments subsequent to remediation actions). Conducting security control assessments in parallel with the development/acquisition and implementation phases of the life cycle permits the identification of weaknesses and deficiencies early and provides the most cost-effective method for initiating corrective actions.

TASK 4-2: Assess the security controls in accordance with the assessment procedures defined in the security assessment plan.

Primary Responsibility: Security Control Assessor

System Development Life Cycle Phase: Development/Acquisition; Implementation.

Security control assessments determine the extent to which the controls are implemented correctly, operating as intended, and producing the desired outcome with respect to meeting the security requirements for the information system. Security control assessments occur as early as practicable in the system development life cycle, preferably during the development phase of the information system.

TASK 4-3: Prepare the security assessment report documenting the issues, findings, and recommendations from the security control assessment.

Primary Responsibility: Security Control Assessor.

System Development Life Cycle Phase: Development/Acquisition; Implementation

The results of the security control assessment, including recommendations for correcting any weaknesses or deficiencies in the controls, are documented in the *security assessment report*. The security assessment report is one of three key documents in the security authorization package developed for authorizing officials. The assessment report includes information from the assessor necessary to determine the effectiveness of the security controls employed within or inherited by the information system based upon the assessor's findings. The security assessment report is an important factor in an authorizing official's determination of risk to organizational operations and assets, individuals, other organizations, and the Nation.

TASK 4-4: Conduct initial remediation actions on security controls based on the findings and recommendations of the security assessment report and reassess remediated control(s), as appropriate.

Primary Responsibility: Information System Owner or Common Control Provider; Security Control Assessor.

System Development Life Cycle Phase: Development/Acquisition; Implementation

References: NIST Special Publications 800-30, 800-53A.

The security assessment report provides visibility into specific weaknesses and deficiencies in the security controls employed within or inherited by the information system that could not reasonably be resolved during system development. The findings generated during the security control assessment facilitate a disciplined and structured approach to mitigating risks in accordance with organizational priorities. Information system owners and common control providers, in collaboration with selected organizational officials (e.g., information system security engineer, authorizing official designated representative, chief information officer, senior information security officer, information owner/steward), may decide that certain findings are inconsequential and present no significant risk to the organization. Alternatively, the organizational officials may decide that certain findings are in fact, significant, requiring immediate remediation actions. In all cases, organizations review assessor findings and determine the severity or seriousness of the findings (i.e., the potential adverse impact on organizational operations and assets, individuals, other organizations, or the Nation) and whether the findings are sufficiently significant to be worthy of further investigation or remediation.

Organizations can prepare an optional addendum to the security assessment report that is transmitted to the authorizing official. The optional addendum provides information system owners and common control providers an opportunity to respond to the initial findings of assessors. The addendum may include, for example, information regarding initial remediation actions taken by information system owners or common control providers in response to assessor findings, or provide an owner's perspective on the findings (e.g., including additional explanatory material, rebutting certain findings, and correcting the record). The addendum to the security assessment report does not change or influence in any manner, the initial assessor findings provided in the original report. Information provided in the addendum is considered by authorizing officials in their risk-based authorization decisions. Organizations may choose to employ an *issue resolution process* to help determine the appropriate actions to take with regard to the security control weaknesses and deficiencies identified during the assessment. Issue resolution can help address vulnerabilities and associated risk, false positives, and other factors that may provide useful information to authorizing officials regarding the security state of the information system including the ongoing effectiveness of system-specific, hybrid, and common controls.

RMF STEP 5 – AUTHORIZE INFORMATION SYSTEM

TASK 5-1: Prepare the plan of action and milestones based on the findings and recommendations of the security assessment report excluding any remediation actions taken.

Primary Responsibility: Information System Owner or Common Control Provider.

System Development Life Cycle Phase: Implementation.

The *plan of action and milestones*, prepared for the authorizing official by the information system owner or the common control provider, is one of three key documents in the security authorization package and describes the specific tasks that are planned: (i) to correct any weaknesses or deficiencies in the security controls noted during the assessment; and (ii) to address the residual vulnerabilities in the information system. The plan of action and milestones identifies: (i) the tasks to be accomplished with a recommendation for completion either before or after information system implementation; (ii) the resources required to accomplish the tasks; (iii) any milestones in meeting the tasks; and (iv) the scheduled completion dates for the milestones. The plan of action and milestones is used by the authorizing official to monitor progress in correcting weaknesses or deficiencies noted during the security control assessment.

TASK 5-2: Assemble the security authorization package and submit the package to the authorizing official for adjudication.

Primary Responsibility: Information System Owner or Common Control Provider.

System Development Life Cycle Phase: Implementation.

The *security authorization package* contains: (i) the security plan; (ii) the security assessment report; and (iii) the plan of action and milestones. The information in these key documents is used by authorizing officials to make risk-based authorization decisions. For information systems inheriting common controls for specific security capabilities, the security authorization package for the common controls or a reference to such documentation is also included in the authorization package. When security controls are provided to an organization by an external provider (e.g., through contracts, interagency agreements, lines of business arrangements, licensing agreements, and/or supply chain arrangements), the organization ensures that the information needed for authorizing officials to make risk based decisions, is made available by the provider.

TASK 5-3: Determine the risk to organizational operations (including mission, functions, image, or reputation), organizational assets, individuals, other organizations, or the Nation.

Primary Responsibility: Authorizing Official or Designated Representative.

References: NIST Special Publications 800-30, 800-39.

System Development Life Cycle Phase: Implementation.

The authorizing official or designated representative, in collaboration with the senior information security officer, assesses the information provided by the information system owner or common control provider regarding the current security state of the system or the common controls inherited by the system and the recommendations for addressing any residual risks. Risk assessments (either formal or informal) are employed at the discretion of the organization to provide needed information on threats, vulnerabilities, and potential impacts as well as the analyses for the risk mitigation recommendations. The risk executive (function) also provides information to the authorizing official that is considered in the final determination of risk to organizational operations and assets, individuals, other organizations, and the Nation resulting from the operation and use of the information system.

TASK 5-4: Determine if the risk to organizational operations, organizational assets, individuals, other organizations, or the Nation is acceptable.

Primary Responsibility: Authorizing Official

System Development Life Cycle Phase: Implementation

References: NIST Special Publication 800-39.

The authorizing official or designated representative, in collaboration with the senior information security officer, assesses the information provided by the information system owner or common control provider regarding the current security state of the system or the common controls inherited by the system and the recommendations for addressing any residual risks. Risk assessments (either formal or informal) are employed at the discretion of the organization to provide needed information on threats, vulnerabilities, and potential impacts as well as the analyses for the risk mitigation recommendations.

RMF STEP 6 – MONITOR SECURITY CONTROLS

TASK 6-1: Determine the security impact of proposed or actual changes to the information system and its environment of operation.

Primary Responsibility: Information System Owner or Common Control Provider.

System Development Life Cycle Phase: Operation/Maintenance.

References: NIST Special Publications 800-30, 800-53A.

Information systems are in a constant state of change with upgrades to hardware, software, or firmware and modifications to the surrounding environments where the systems reside and operate. A disciplined and structured approach to managing, controlling, and documenting changes to an information system or its environment of operation is an essential element of an effective security control monitoring program.

TASK 6-2: Assess a selected subset of the technical, management, and operational security controls employed within and inherited by the information system in accordance with the organization-defined monitoring strategy.

Primary Responsibility: Security Control Assessor

System Development Life Cycle Phase: Operation/Maintenance.

References: NIST Special Publication 800-53A.

Organizations assess all security controls employed within and inherited by the information system during the initial security authorization. Subsequent to the initial authorization, the organization assesses a subset of the security controls (including management, operational, and technical controls) on an ongoing basis during continuous monitoring. The selection of appropriate security controls to monitor and the frequency of monitoring are based on the monitoring strategy developed by the information system owner or common control provider and approved by the authorizing official and senior information security officer.

TASK 6-3: Conduct remediation actions based on the results of ongoing monitoring activities, assessment of risk, and outstanding items in the plan of action and milestones.

Primary Responsibility: Information System Owner or Common Control Provider

System Development Life Cycle Phase: Operation/Maintenance.

References: NIST Special Publications 800-30, 800-53, 800-53A; CNSS Instruction 1253.

The assessment information produced by an assessor during continuous monitoring is provided to the information system owner and common control provider in an updated *security assessment report*. The information system owner and common control provider initiate remediation actions on outstanding items listed in the plan of actions and milestones and findings produced during the ongoing monitoring of security controls.

TASK 6-4: Update the security plan, security assessment report, and plan of action and milestones based on the results of the continuous monitoring process.

Primary Responsibility: Information System Owner or Common Control Provider.

System Development Life Cycle Phase: Operation/Maintenance.

References: NIST Special Publication 800-53A.

To facilitate the near real-time management of risk associated with the operation and use of the information system, the organization updates the security plan, security assessment report, and plan of action and milestones on an ongoing basis. The updated security plan reflects any modifications to security controls based on risk mitigation activities carried out by the information system owner or common control provider.

TASK 6-5: Report the security status of the information system (including the effectiveness of security controls employed within and inherited by the system) to the authorizing official and other appropriate organizational officials on an ongoing basis in accordance with the monitoring strategy.

Primary Responsibility: Information System Owner or Common Control Provider.

System Development Life Cycle Phase: Operation/Maintenance.

References: NIST Special Publication 800-53A.

The results of monitoring activities are recorded and reported to the authorizing official on an ongoing basis in accordance with the monitoring strategy. Security status reporting can be: (i) event-driven (e.g., when the information system or its environment of operation changes or the system is compromised or breached); (ii) time-driven (e.g., weekly, monthly, quarterly); or (iii) both (event- and time-driven). Security status reports provide the authorizing official and other senior leaders within the organization, essential information with regard to the security state of the information system including the effectiveness of deployed security controls. Security status reports describe the ongoing monitoring activities employed by the information system owner or common control provider.

TASK 6-6: Review the reported security status of the information system (including the effectiveness of security controls employed within and inherited by the system) on an ongoing basis in accordance with the monitoring strategy to determine whether the risk to organizational operations, organizational assets, individuals, other organizations, or the Nation remains acceptable.

Primary Responsibility: Authorizing Official.

System Development Life Cycle Phase: Operation/Maintenance.

The authorizing official or designated representative reviews the reported security status of the information system (including the effectiveness of deployed security controls) on an ongoing basis, to determine the current risk to organizational operations and assets, individuals, other organizations, or the Nation. The authorizing official determines, with inputs as appropriate from the authorizing official designated representative, senior information security officer, and the risk executive (function), whether the current risk is acceptable and forwards appropriate direction to the information system owner or common control provider.

TASK 6-7: Implement an information system decommissioning strategy, when needed, which executes required actions when a system is removed from service.

Primary Responsibility: Information System Owner.

System Development Life Cycle Phase: Disposal.

References: NIST Special Publications 800-30, 800-53A.

When a federal information system is removed from operation, a number of risk management related actions are required. Organizations ensure that all security controls addressing information system removal and decommissioning (e.g., media sanitization, configuration management and control) are implemented. Organizational tracking and management systems (including inventory systems) are updated to indicate the specific information system components that are being removed from service

RMF Roles and Responsibilities

D.1 HEAD OF AGENCY (CHIEF EXECUTIVE OFFICER)

The head of agency (or chief executive officer) is the highest-level senior official or executive within an organization with the overall responsibility to provide information security protections commensurate with the risk and magnitude of harm (i.e., impact) to organizational operations and assets, individuals, other organizations, and the Nation resulting from unauthorized access, use, disclosure, disruption, modification, or destruction of: (i) information collected or maintained by or on behalf of the agency; and (ii) information systems used or operated by an agency or by a contractor of an agency or other organization on behalf of an agency.

D.2 RISK EXECUTIVE (FUNCTION)

The risk executive (function) is an individual or group within an organization that helps to ensure that: (i) risk-related considerations for individual information systems, to include authorization decisions, are viewed from an organization-wide perspective with regard to the overall strategic goals and objectives of the organization in carrying out its core missions and business functions; and (ii) managing information system-related security risks is consistent across the organization, reflects organizational risk tolerance, and is considered along with other types of risks in order to ensure mission/business success

D.3 CHIEF INFORMATION OFFICER

The chief information officer is an organizational official responsible for: (i) designating a senior information security officer; (ii) developing and maintaining information security policies, procedures, and control techniques to address all applicable requirements; (iii) overseeing personnel with significant responsibilities for information security and ensuring that the personnel are adequately trained; (iv) assisting senior organizational officials concerning their security responsibilities; and (v) in coordination with other senior officials, reporting annually to the head of the federal agency on the overall effectiveness of the organization's information security program, including progress of remedial actions.

D.4 INFORMATION OWNER/STEWARD

The *information owner/steward* is an organizational official with statutory, management, or operational authority for specified information and the responsibility for establishing the policies and procedures governing its generation, collection, processing, dissemination, and disposal. In information-sharing environments, the information owner/steward is responsible for establishing the rules for appropriate use and protection of the subject information (e.g., rules of behavior) and retains that responsibility even when the information is shared with or provided to other organizations.

D.5 SENIOR INFORMATION SECURITY OFFICER

The *senior information security officer* is an organizational official responsible for: (i) carrying out the chief information officer security responsibilities under FISMA; and (ii) serving as the primary liaison for the chief information officer to the organization's authorizing officials, information system owners, common control providers, and information system security officers.

D.6 AUTHORIZING OFFICIAL

The *authorizing official* is a senior official or executive with the authority to formally assume responsibility for operating an information system at an acceptable level of risk to organizational operations and assets, individuals, other organizations, and the Nation Authorizing officials typically have budgetary oversight for an information system *or* are responsible for the mission and/or business operations supported by the system. Through the security authorization process, authorizing officials are *accountable* for the security risks associated with information system operations. Accordingly, authorizing officials are in management positions with a level of authority commensurate with understanding and accepting such information system-related security risks.

D.7 AUTHORIZING OFFICIAL DESIGNATED REPRESENTATIVE

The *authorizing official designated representative* is an organizational official that acts on behalf of an authorizing official to coordinate and conduct the required day-to-day activities associated with the security authorization process. The only activity that cannot be delegated to the designated representative by the authorizing official is the authorization decision and signing of the associated authorization decision document

D.8 COMMON CONTROL PROVIDER

The *common control provider* is an individual, group, or organization responsible for the development, implementation, assessment, and monitoring of common controls (i.e., security controls inherited by information systems).

D.9 INFORMATION SYSTEM OWNER

The *information system owner* is an organizational official responsible for the procurement, development, integration, modification, operation, maintenance, and disposal of an information system.

D.10 INFORMATION SYSTEM SECURITY OFFICER

The *information system security officer* is an individual responsible for ensuring that the appropriate operational security posture is maintained for an information system and as such, works in close collaboration with the information system owner. The information system security officer also serves as a principal advisor on all matters, technical and otherwise, involving the security of an information system.

D.11 INFORMATION SECURITY ARCHITECT

The *information security architect* is an individual, group, or organization responsible for ensuring that the information security requirements necessary to protect the organization's core missions and business processes are adequately addressed in all aspects of enterprise architecture including reference models, segment and solution architectures, and the resulting information systems supporting those missions and business processes. The information security architect serves as the liaison between the enterprise architect and the information system security engineer

D.12 INFORMATION SYSTEM SECURITY ENGINEER

The *information system security engineer* is an individual, group, or organization responsible for conducting information system security engineering activities. Information system security engineering is a process that captures and refines information security requirements and ensures that the requirements are effectively integrated into information technology component products and information systems through purposeful security architecting, design, development, and configuration.

D.13 SECURITY CONTROL ASSESSOR

The *security control assessor* is an individual, group, or organization responsible for conducting a comprehensive assessment of the management, operational, and technical security controls employed within or inherited by an information system to determine the overall effectiveness of the controls (i.e., the extent to which the controls are implemented correctly, operating as intended, and producing the desired outcome with respect to meeting the security requirements for the system)

5 SYSTEM DEVELOPMENT LIFE CYCLE (SDLC) AND RMF

SLDC

To be most effective, information security must be integrated into the SDLC from system inception. Early integration of security in the SDLC enables agencies to maximize return on investment in their security programs, through:

-Early identification and mitigation of security vulnerabilities and misconfigurations, resulting in lower cost of security control implementation and vulnerability mitigation;
-Awareness of potential engineering challenges caused by mandatory security controls;
-Identification of shared security services and reuse of security strategies and tools to reduce development cost and schedule while improving security posture through proven methods and techniques; and
-Facilitation of informed executive decision making through comprehensive risk management in a timely manner.
A typical SDLC includes five phases: initiation, development/acquisition, implementation/assessment, operations/maintenance, and disposal. Each phase includes a minimum set of security tasks needed to effectively incorporate security in the system development process. Note that phases may continue to be repeated throughout a system's life prior to disposal.

-*Initiation*. During the initiation phase, the need for a system is expressed and the purpose of the system is documented.
-*Development/Acquisition*. During this phase, the system is designed, purchased, programmed, developed, or otherwise constructed.
-*Implementation/Assessment*. After system acceptance testing, the system is installed or fielded.
-*Operation/Maintenance*. During this phase, the system performs its work. The system is almost always modified by the addition of hardware and software and by numerous other events.
-*Disposal*. Activities conducted during this phase ensure the orderly termination of the system, safeguarding vital system information, and migrating data processed by the system to a new system, or preserving it in accordance with applicable records management regulations and policies.

RMF and SDLC relationship

SDLC Phases	RMF	RMF Documents
Initiation	Categorize Tasks 1, 2, 3 Select Tasks 1, 2, 3	
Acquisition/Development	Select Task 4 Implement Tasks 1, 2 Assess Tasks 1, 2, 3, 4	SSP
Implementation/Assessment	Implement Tasks 1, 2 Assess Tasks 1, 2, 3, 4 Authorize Tasks 1, 2, 3, 4	SAR POAM Authorization package
Operation/Maintenance	Monitor Tasks 1, 2, 3, 4, 5	
Disposal	Monitor Task 6	Status Reports

6 INFORMATION CATEGORIZATION

Information Types and Information System Categorization

FIPS Publication 199 defines three levels of *potential impact* on organizations or individuals should there be a breach of security (i.e., a loss of confidentiality, integrity, or availability). The application of these definitions must take place within the context of each organization and the overall national interest.

The *potential impact* is **LOW** if—
− The loss of confidentiality, integrity, or availability could be expected to have a **limited** adverse effect on organizational operations, organizational assets, or individuals.

The *potential impact* is **MODERATE** if—
− The loss of confidentiality, integrity, or availability could be expected to have a **serious** adverse effect on organizational operations, organizational assets, or individuals

The *potential impact* is **HIGH** if—
− The loss of confidentiality, integrity, or availability could be expected to have a **severe or catastrophic** adverse effect on organizational operations, organizational assets, or individuals.

The generalized format for expressing the security <u>category, SC, of an information type</u> is:
SC information type = {(**confidentiality**, *impact*), (**integrity**, *impact*), (**availability**, *impact*)}, where the acceptable values for potential impact are LOW, MODERATE, HIGH, or NOT APPLICABLE

<u>Determining the security category of an information system</u> requires slightly more analysis and must consider the security categories of all information types resident on the information system. For an information system, the potential impact values assigned to the respective security objectives (confidentiality, integrity, availability) shall be the highest values <u>(i.e., high water mark) from</u> among those security categories that have been determined for each type of information resident on the information system.

The generalized format for expressing the security category, SC, of an information system is:
SC information system = {(**confidentiality**, *impact*), (**integrity**, *impact*), (**availability**, *impact*)}, where the acceptable values for potential impact are LOW, MODERATE, or HIGH.

<u>Note that the value of *not applicable* cannot be assigned to any security objective in the context of establishing a security category for an information system.</u>

<u>Since the impact values (i.e., levels) for confidentiality, integrity, and availability may not always be the same for a particular information system, the high water mark concept is used to determine the overall impact level of the information system.</u> The security impact level for an information system will generally be the highest impact level for the security objectives (confidentiality, integrity, and availability) associated with the aggregate of system information types. Thus, a low-impact system is defined as an information system in which all three of the security objectives are low. A moderate-impact system is an information system in which at least one of the security objectives is moderate and no security objective is greater than moderate. And finally, a high-impact system is an information system in which at least one security objective is high.

Categorization Process Diagram

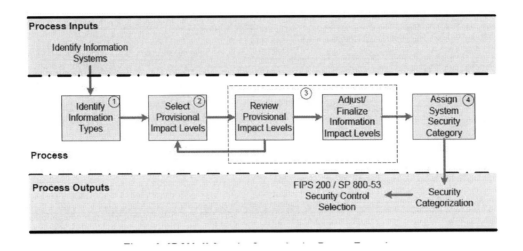

7 SECURITY CONTROLS

Security Control Families and Baselines

800-53: Security controls have a well-defined organization and structure. For ease of use in the security control selection and specification process, controls are organized into **eighteen *families***. Each family contains security controls related to the general security topic of the family. A two-character identifier uniquely identifies security control families, for example, PS (Personnel Security). Security controls may involve aspects of policy, oversight, supervision, manual processes, actions by individuals, or automated mechanisms implemented by information systems/devices.

To assist organizations in making the appropriate selection of security controls for information systems, the concept of *baseline* controls is introduced. Baseline controls are the starting point for the security control selection process. 800-53 Appendix D provides a listing of the security control baselines. Three security control baselines have been identified corresponding to the low-impact, moderate-impact, and high-impact information systems using the high water mark defined in FIPS Publication 200 and used in Section 3.1 of 800-53 to provide an initial set of security controls for each impact level.

Types of Controls

There are three distinct types of designations related to the security controls that define: (i) the scope of applicability for the control; (ii) the shared nature of the control; and (iii) the responsibility for control development, implementation, assessment, and authorization. These designations include *common* controls, *system-specific* controls, and *hybrid* controls.

Common controls are security controls whose implementation results in a security capability that is *inheritable* by one or more organizational information systems. Security controls are deemed inheritable by information systems or information system components when the systems or components receive protection from the implemented controls but the controls are developed, implemented, assessed, authorized, and monitored by entities other than those responsible for the systems or components—entities internal or external to the organizations where the systems or components reside.

The identification of common controls is most effectively accomplished as an organization-wide exercise with the active involvement of chief information officers, senior information security officers, the risk executive (function), authorizing officials, information owners/stewards, information system owners, and information system security officers. The organization-wide exercise considers the security categories of the information systems within the organization and the security controls necessary to adequately mitigate the risks arising from the use of those systems

Security controls not designated as common controls are considered *system-specific* or *hybrid* controls. System-specific controls are the primary responsibility of information system owners and their respective authorizing officials. Organizations assign a *hybrid* status to security controls when one part of the control is common and another part of the control is system-specific. For example, an organization may choose to implement the Incident Response Policy and Procedures security control (IR-1) as a hybrid control with the policy portion of the control designated as common and the procedures portion of the control designated as system-specific. Hybrid controls may also serve as predefined templates for further control refinement. Organizations may choose, for example, to implement the Contingency Planning security control (CP-2) as a predefined template for a generalized contingency plan for all organizational information systems with information system owners tailoring the plan, where appropriate, for system-specific uses

External Providers

FISMA and OMB policies require that federal agencies using external service providers to process, store, or transmit federal information or operate information systems on behalf of the federal government, assure that such use meets the same security requirements that federal agencies are required to meet. Security requirements for external service providers including the security controls for external information systems are expressed in contracts or other formal agreements. Organizations are responsible and accountable for the information security risk incurred by the use of information system services provided by external providers. Such risk is addressed by incorporating the Risk Management Framework (RMF) as part of the terms and conditions of the contracts with external providers. Organizations can require external providers to implement all steps in the RMF except the security authorization step, which remains an inherent federal responsibility directly linked to managing the information security risk related to the use of external information system services

Tailoring/Scoping/Compensating

After selecting the applicable security control baseline from Appendix D, organizations initiate the tailoring process to modify appropriately and align the controls more closely with the specific conditions within the organization (i.e., conditions related to organizational missions/business functions, information systems, or environments of operation). The tailoring process includes:
• Identifying and designating common controls in initial security control baselines;
• Applying scoping considerations to the remaining baseline security controls;
• Selecting compensating security controls, if needed

• Assigning specific values to organization-defined security control parameters via explicit assignment and selection statements;
• Supplementing baselines with additional security controls and control enhancements, if needed; and
• Providing additional specification information for control implementation, if needed.

The application of scoping considerations can eliminate unnecessary security controls from the initial security control baselines and help to ensure that organizations select *only* those controls that are needed to provide the appropriate level of protection for organizational information systems—protection based on the missions and business functions being supported by those systems and the environments in which the systems operate.

Organizations may find it necessary on occasion to employ compensating security controls. Compensating controls are alternative security controls employed by organizations in lieu of specific controls in the low, moderate, or high baselines described in 800-53 Appendix D—controls that provide equivalent or comparable protection for organizational information systems and the information processed, stored, or transmitted by those systems. This may occur, for example, when organizations are unable to effectively implement specific security controls in the baselines or when, due to the specific nature of the information systems or environments of operation, the controls in the baselines are not a cost-effective means of obtaining the needed risk mitigation. Compensating controls are typically selected after applying the scoping considerations in the tailoring guidance to the applicable security control baseline

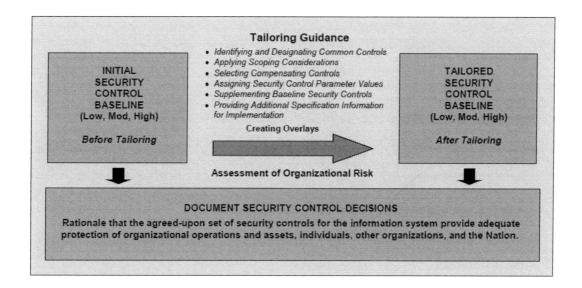

Overlays

To address the need for developing community-wide and specialized sets of security controls for information systems and organizations, the concept of *overlay* is introduced. An overlay is a fully specified set of security controls, control enhancements, and supplemental guidance derived from the application of tailoring guidance.

8 RISK ANALYSIS AND ASSESSMENT

Vulnerability/Threat

A threat is any circumstance or event with the potential to adversely impact organizational operations and assets, individuals, other organizations, or the Nation through an information system via unauthorized access, destruction, disclosure, or modification of information, and/or denial of service. Threat events are caused by threat sources. A threat source is characterized as: (i) the intent and method targeted at the exploitation of a vulnerability; or (ii) a situation and method that may accidentally exploit a vulnerability. In general, types of threat sources include: (i) hostile cyber or physical attacks; (ii) human errors of omission or commission; (iii) structural failures of organization-controlled resources (e.g., hardware, software, environmental controls); and (iv) natural and man-made disasters, accidents, and failures beyond the control of the organization.

A vulnerability is a weakness in an information system, system security procedures, internal controls, or implementation that could be exploited by a threat source.25Most information system vulnerabilities can be associated with security controls that either have not been applied (either intentionally or unintentionally), or have been applied, but retain some weakness. However, it is also important to allow for the possibility of emergent vulnerabilities that can arise naturally over time as organizational missions/business functions evolve, environments of operation change, new technologies proliferate, and new threats emerge. In the context of such change, existing security controls may become inadequate and may need to be reassessed for effectiveness. The tendency for security controls to potentially degrade in effectiveness over time reinforces the need to maintain risk assessments during the entire system development life cycle and also the importance of continuous monitoring programs to obtain ongoing situational awareness of the organizational security posture.

Likelihood/Impact

The likelihood of occurrence is a weighted risk factor based on an analysis of the probability that a given threat is capable of exploiting a given vulnerability (or set of vulnerabilities). The likelihood risk factor combines an estimate of the likelihood that the threat event will be initiated with an estimate of the likelihood of impact (i.e., the likelihood that the threat event results in adverse impacts). For adversarial threats, an assessment of likelihood of occurrence is typically based on: (i) adversary intent; (ii) adversary capability; and (iii) adversary targeting.

The level of impact from a threat event is the magnitude of harm that can be expected to result from the consequences of unauthorized disclosure of information, unauthorized modification of information, unauthorized destruction of information, or loss of information or information system availability. Such harm can be experienced by a variety of organizational and non-organizational stakeholders including, for example, heads of agencies, mission and business owners, information owners/stewards, mission/business process owners, information system owners, or individuals/groups in the public or private sectors relying on the organization—in essence, anyone with a vested interest in the organization's operations, assets, or individuals, including other organizations in partnership with the organization, or the Nation.

Risk Analysis Approaches

Analysis approaches differ with respect to the orientation or starting point of the risk assessment, level of detail in the assessment, and how risks due to similar threat scenarios are treated. An analysis approach can be: (i) *threat-oriented*; (ii) *asset/impact-oriented*; or (iii) *vulnerability-oriented*.

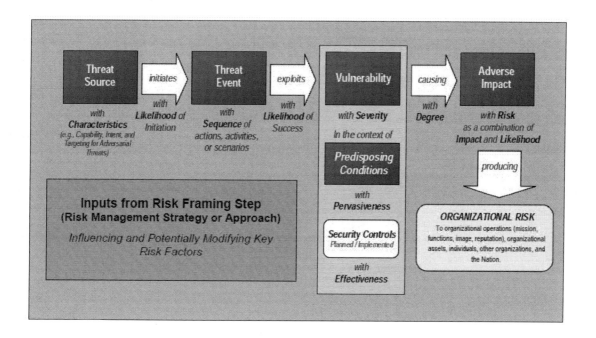

Risk Assessment Process

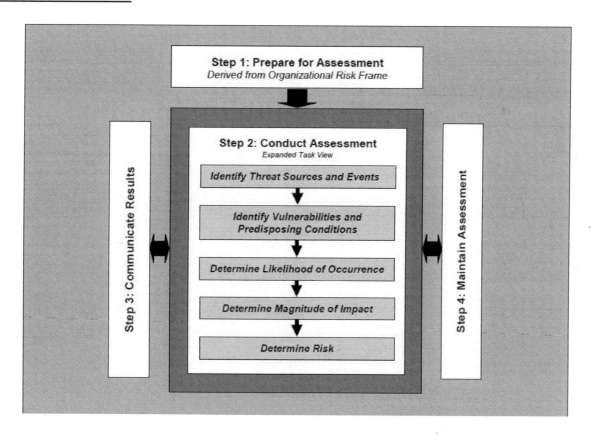

Risk Assessment Computation Table (Likelihood – Impact)

Likelihood (Threat Event Occurs and Results in Adverse Impact)	Level of Impact				
	Very Low	Low	Moderate	High	Very High
Very High	Very Low	Low	Moderate	High	Very High
High	Very Low	Low	Moderate	High	Very High
Moderate	Very Low	Low	Moderate	Moderate	High
Low	Very Low	Low	Low	Low	Moderate
Very Low	Very Low	Very Low	Very Low	Low	Low

Trust and Assurance

Trustworthiness with respect to information systems, expresses the degree to which the systems can be expected to preserve with some degree of confidence, the confidentiality, integrity, and availability of the information that is being processed, stored, or transmitted by the systems across a range of threats. Trustworthy information systems are systems that are believed to be capable of operating within a defined risk tolerance

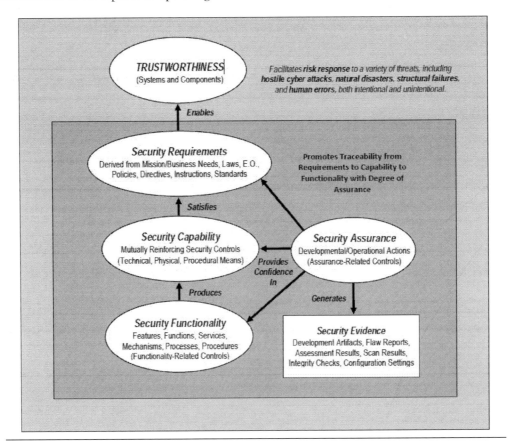

Controls Assessment Fundamental Concepts

An assessment procedure consists of a set of assessment *objectives*, each with an associated set of potential assessment *methods* and assessment *objects*. An assessment objective includes a set of *determination statements* related to the security control under assessment

Assessment objects identify the specific items being assessed and include *specifications*, *mechanisms*, *activities*, and *individuals*. Specifications are the document-based artifacts (e.g., policies, procedures, plans, system security requirements, functional specifications, and architectural designs) associated with an information system. Mechanisms are the specific hardware, software, or firmware safeguards and countermeasures employed within an information system. Activities are the specific protection-related pursuits or actions supporting an information system that involve people (e.g., conducting system backup operations, monitoring network traffic, exercising a contingency plan). Individuals, or groups of individuals, are people applying the specifications, mechanisms, or activities described above.

Assessment methods define the nature of the assessor actions and include *examine*, *interview*, and *test*. The *examine* method is the process of reviewing, inspecting, observing, studying, or analyzing one or more assessment objects (i.e., specifications, mechanisms, or activities). The purpose of the examine method is to facilitate assessor understanding, achieve clarification, or obtain evidence. The *interview* method is the process of holding discussions with individuals or groups of individuals within an organization to once again, facilitate assessor understanding, achieve clarification, or obtain evidence. The *test* method is the process of exercising one or more assessment objects (i.e., activities or mechanisms) under specified conditions to compare actual with expected behavior. In all three assessment methods, the results are used in making specific determinations called for in the determination statements and thereby achieving the objectives for the assessment procedure.

The assessment methods have a set of associated attributes, *depth* and *coverage*, which help define the level of effort for the assessment. The depth attribute addresses the rigor of and level of detail in the examination, interview, and testing processes. Values for the depth attribute include *basic*, *focused*, and *comprehensive*. The coverage attribute addresses the scope or breadth of the examination, interview, and testing processes including the number and type of specifications, mechanisms, and activities to be examined or tested and the number and types of individuals to be interviewed. Similar to the depth attribute, values for the coverage attribute include *basic*, *focused*, and *comprehensive*.

Information Security Continuous Monitoring (ISCM) - how often?

ISCM in support of ongoing assessment and authorization has the potential to be resource intensive and time-consuming. It is impractical to collect security-related information and assess every aspect of every security control deployed across an organization at all times. A more practical approach is to establish reasonable assessment frequencies for collecting security-related information. The frequency of assessments should be sufficient to assure adequate security commensurate with risk

An organization's ISCM strategy also changes as the organization's security program(s) and monitoring capabilities mature. In a fully mature program, security-related information collection and analysis are accomplished using standardized methods across the organization, as an integral part of mission and business processes, and automated to the fullest extent possible. In this case, the security program is mature enough to ensure that sufficient processes and procedures effectively secure the enterprise architecture in accordance with organizational risk tolerances, and to collect, correlate, analyze, and report on relevant security metrics.

ABOUT THE AUTHOR

David Boone (pseudonym) is an experienced security professional working away keeping systems secure and contributing daily to authorization related tasks

91011619R00022

Made in the USA
Middletown, DE
27 September 2018